Five Rings of Kung Fu

Go Rin No Sho for the Martial Arts

Sifu Hou San

Five Rings of Kung Fu:

Go Rin No Sho for the Martial Arts

Copyright 2017 Sifu Hou San

All rights are expressly reserved unless otherwise noted. No part of this book may be reproduced or copied by any means without written permission from the author.

ISBN 978-1-387-55015-9

The author assumes no responsibility for misuse of any information included in this book.

Table of Contents

Five Rings of Kung Fu 1

Author's Introduction 5

What are the Five Rings? 6

Wu Hsing 9

The Pentagram in Chinese Mysticism 10

The Creative Cycle 12

The Destructive Cycle 14

The Five Animals of Kung Fu 16

Introduction 19

The Ground Book 22

The Water Book 40

The Fire Book 61

The Wind Book 82

The Book of the Void 94

Author's Introduction

Miyamoto Musashi was born 1584 – June 13. At the age of sixty he retired from his life of duels to discover the meaning to his art. The result was "The Book of Five Rings." Millions of copies have been purchased worldwide by everyone from businessmen to martial artists. The wisdom of this book is no doubt useful as a strategy guide to many but there are truly few who can apply its wisdom to their art. This is especially true of those who do not practice the sword but arts such as Kung Fu or Karate. In this book I have included commentary discussing how to apply the Book of Five Rings to Kung Fu and other martial arts to hopefully give the reader a direction in understanding their own martial art better.

What are the Five Rings?

In Mushashi's Go Rin No Sho, he refers to the chapters as "five rings." These are referring to the five elements used Buddhist teachings. They explain in Buddhist thought the creation cycle of the universe, a person's transition through various stages to enlightenment, and among many other things our psychological makeup and emotions. This blueprint is used also in Ninjutsu to categorize the system's art which is taught on three main levels. Those of mind, body, and spirit. It is also used in Buddhist based Chinese martial arts. The five elements in Taoist arts are based on Wood, Fire, Water, Earth, and Metal. Each of these five levels also can be broken down to positive and negative influence. Sometimes called In and Yo in Japanese or Yin and Yang in Taoist thought. A brief explanation of this is below.

Earth

1.Chi which means Earth, represents energies in a solid state. The most basic example of *chi* is in a mountain. Mountains are resistant to movement or change. In our bodies, the bones, muscles and tissues are represented by *Earth*. On a mental level chi can mean total unmovable confidence. Or in a negative state, it can mean stubbornness. It is a desire to have things remain as they are; a resistance to change. In martial arts it will represent the training of the physical body, developing strength and stamina. Another application would be building the solid foundation of our basics in martial arts upon which all of our advanced techniques are built.

Water

2.Sui or meaning "Water" represents of a fluid or flexible nature. Those of "adaptability." Such as mental or emotional tendencies towards adaptation and change. Water can be associated with emotion, defensiveness, and adaptability. In our training it represents flexibility of body and mind.

Fire

3.Ka "Fire" represents the energetic, forceful, explosive movement. It represents power and aggression. At this stage of training, our skills are done realistically with the attitude of winning no matter what. "I will not lose."

Wind

Fu "Wind" represents wisdom and benevolence. It will show up in our training as being at the right place at the right time and our skills have become effortless. There is no longer a need for power or aggression as our skills are more perfect and our confidence has grown.

Void

5. Kū or "Void", sometime means "sky" or "Heaven." It represents creativity and understanding. At this point skills are perfected and no longer thought about. Our movements come as they are needed naturally without thought. We now have an understanding of our art and are creative in our training and applying our skills. We can now do this at will. Sometimes the void may be thought of as God which created the universe or other four elements. So the void can represent a spiritual path of whatever you happen to believe in. The five elements in Taoist arts are called Wu Hsing or "The Five Agents."

Wu Hsing

Wu Hsing is the theory of the five elements or agents. Wu means five and Hsing means energy or motion. This theory is different from the elemental theory from Greece as it deals more with the transformation of energy rather than static material. It is thought that Wu Hsing in its earliest form was around 500 BC Mongolia and was later systemized around 320 BC by a Chinese scholar named Tsu Yen during the warring states period. The names of each of the five elements in this theory were used as codes representing the action of each element and also its manifestation in nature. These names are as follows:

Earth: nourishes through sowing and reaping.
Water: moistens and descends.
Fire: heats and moves upward.
Wood: can be shaped straight or curved.
Metal: can be melted and then hardened.

The Pentagram in Chinese Mysticism

What we will discuss here is the use of the pentagram as it is used in the Chinese Taoist thought and martial arts. In diagram one its meaning is hidden as all of the lines are drawn in one continuous movement and all we see is a pentagram surrounded by a circle. In reality the pentagram in Chinese mysticism is a series of lines representing the movement of one element to the next of the Chinese Wu Hsing or five element theory. This star-like pattern shows what the Chinese call the "Destruction Cycle." The circle surrounding the star like pattern represents what is called the "Creative Cycle". Shown in its true form, the pattern looks like diagram 2, which shows interaction and changes between the five elements listed earlier in this chapter.

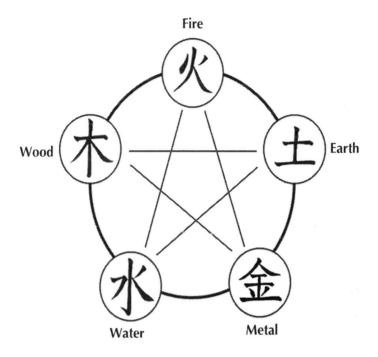

Diagram of the five elements

The Creative Cycle

The circle on diagram 2 is moving in a clockwise direction, showing how each element creates the one after it and in return, is created by the one before. This is called the "Mother/Son" law. At the top of the circle is the element of fire. It is considered to be the mother of earth. Earth is then considered the son of fire. This cycle continues in a clockwise direction with earth, creating metal, metal, creating water, and so on. This continues around the circle in a never- ending cycle. It is most apparent in our yearly seasons:

Wood: Spring
Fire: Summer
Earth: Indian summer
Metal: Fall
Water: Winter

These five elements can be applied to our martial arts as well. If a martial arts system does not contain all five elements it is considered to be imbalanced and can be harmful to the health of the practitioner. These apply to punches as well as kicking techniques.

Metal: strikes downward from above like an ax
Punch: Knife hand or hammer fist downward
Kick: Axe kicks or downward heel
Water: explodes upward like a geyser
Punch: Uppercuts
Kick: Upward swing kicks or knee
Wood: striking forward, crushing
Punch: Straight forward punches
Kicks: Front snap or front heel
Fire: punching forward with a deflection
Punch: Simultaneous block and punch
Kick: Scissors or Crane leaping kick. "One two kick."
Earth: crosses the line of attack from side to side
Punch: Inward hammer fist, outward and downward blocks.
Kicks: Crescent or half-moon kicks. Inside or outside.

Using the Japanese five elemental theories we can see the five elements even in death.

Void: the spirit leaves the body
Wind: the breath leaves the body
Fire: heat leaves the body
Water: the body tissues dry up
Earth: the body returns to dust

The Destructive Cycle

Fire: destroys metal by melting
Metal: destroys wood by chopping
Wood: destroys Earth by splitting
Earth: destroys water by damming
Water: destroys fire by extinguishing

This cycle is known as the "Grandmother/Son" law. The grandmother is the parent of the son's mother on the chart. In Chinese medicine, it is usually the grandmother that is attacking the son or associated element causing illness and bad health. These elemental/organ associations are listed here.

Wood-Liver, Gallbladder
Fire- Heart, Small Intestine
Earth-Spleen, Stomach
Metal-Lungs, Large Intestines
Water-Bladder, Kidneys

The organ listed directly to the right of the element is considered "Yin." The organs listed to the right are "Yang." They are listed in this way according to whether the organ is considered solid or hollow. The ones considered hollow, empty themselves of any fluid that they contain. For example the kidneys filter blood and water and then emptying this fluid into the bladder.

According to the Mother/Son law, the heart would send its blood or chi to the spleen, which in return sends its chi to the lungs. If the chi of the heart is too strong, then its son or the spleen would be affected and the heart would need to be sedated or have its chi weakened thereby creating less stress on the spleen. This is a small example of what the creative cycle represented by the circle means. An example of the Grandmother/Son law would be the liver having too much chi, which would indirectly affect the lungs. This is shown in the star section of the chart shown earlier. Through diagnosis using these charts, any imbalances of chi in the organs would be handled through the use of herbs, acupuncture, and special breathing exercises called "Qigong."

This energy called chi travels along the body in what are called meridians. These meridians travel along the surface of the skin, bone and muscle, creating a three-dimensional energy body. On each of these meridian lines are points that can be used to stimulate or sedate the energy running through them to the internal organs. This energy body can be seen in plants using Kirlian photography. When the plant dies this energy body no longer shows up. It is this energy and the two cycles mentioned earlier that are used in Chinese medicine.

The Five Animals of Kung Fu

Before the Shaolin temple began to train Kungfu, the temples were much like the Catholic monasteries of Europe. It was a place for meditation and translating the Sanskrit scriptures into the Chinese language so that the local population could learn and practice Buddhism. But this practice was leaving the monks tired and weak. In approximately 520 A.D., an Indian monk named Bodhi dharma came to the Shaolin temple to teach the Eight Fold Path and seeing the weakened state of the monks, he taught them an exercise called the "Eighteen Lohan". These eighteen exercises mimicked the movements of animals, and are thought to have originated from Indian yoga. Bodhi dharma was of the warrior caste in India, and so may have brought with him martial techniques as well. The monks began to notice that this training greatly enhanced their strength, so it was later continued alongside their practice of Kungfu.

From these eighteen exercises, many styles of Kungfu were developed mimicking the movements of animals that were seen in the areas around the temple. Some of the animal systems that were created were Crane, Tiger, Snake, Monkey and Praying Mantis. Other systems were created after mythical creatures such as the Dragon and Phoenix.

The more famous animal systems of the Shaolin temple were Tiger, Dragon, Crane, Snake, and Leopard. These five animal systems represent the mind and the body of the practitioner. Together they were called the "Five Animal Style". Training the five animal style is for developing a strong body and spirit in the practitioner. The word spirit in Kungfu means your outlook on life and your ability to face hardships without fear or doubt. Below are the benefits of training each of these five animal styles.

Tiger: Strengthens the bone structure
Crane: Strengthens the sinew
Leopard: Strengthens the muscles
Snake: Develops the chi or internal energy
Dragon: Creates a strong spirit

The elements in Taoist arts came from Mongolia. Wu Hsing is the theory of the five elements or agents. Wu means five and Hsing means energy or motion. This theory is different from the elemental theory from Greece as it deals more with the transformation of energy rather than static material. It is thought that Wu Hsing in its earliest form was around 500 BC Mongolia and was later systemized around 320 BC by a Chinese scholar named

Tsu Yen during the warring states period. The names of each of the five elements in this theory were used as codes representing the action of each element and also its manifestation in nature. These names are as follows:

    Earth: nourishes through sowing and reaping.
    Water: moistens and descends.
    Fire: heats and moves upward.
    Wood: can be shaped straight or curved.
    Metal: can be melted and then hardened.

Although the elements connected to the five animals are the Chinese version, I will try to compare them later to the Japanese version of the elements or "Five Rings." These animal elements are used in Shaolin and Hung Gar Kung Fu as well. And are as below.

Dragon: Fire, Tiger: Wood, Crane: Earth, Leopard: Metal, Snake: Water.

Introduction

I have been many years training in the Way of strategy called Ni Ten Ichi Ryu, and now I think I will explain it in writing for the first time. It is now during the first ten days of the tenth month in the twentieth year of Kanei (1645). I have climbed mountain Iwato of Higoin Kyushu to pay homage to heaven," pray to Kwannon," and kneel before Buddha. I am a warrior of Harima province, Shinmen Musashi No Kami Fujiwara No Geshin, age sixty years.

From youth my heart has been inclined toward the Way of strategy. My first duel was when I was thirteen; I struck down a strategist of the Shinto school, one Arima Kihei. When I was sixteen I struck down an able strategist, Tadashima Akiyama. When I was twenty-one I went up to the capital and met all manner of strategists, never once failing to win in many contests.

After that I went from province to province dueling with strategists of various schools, and not once failed to win even though I had as many as sixty encounters. This was between the ages of thirteen and twenty-eight or twenty-nine.

When I reached thirty I looked back on my past. The previous victories were not due to my having mastered strategy. Perhaps it was natural ability, or the order of heaven, or that other schools' strategy was inferior. After that I studied morning and evening searching for the principle, and came to realize the Way of strategy when I was fifty.

Since then I have lived without following any particular Way. Thus with the virtue of strategy I practice many arts and abilities all things with no teacher. To write this book I did neither use the law of Buddha or the teachings of Confucius, neither old war chronicles nor books on martial tactics. I take up my brush to explain the true spirit of this Ichi school as it is mirrored in the Way of heaven and Kwannon. The time is the night of the tenth day of the tenth month, at the hour of the tiger. (3-5 a.m.)

Musashi's introduction to the Book of Five Rings gives us the following:

1. His love for training and the warrior life.
2. The duels he fought.
3. His reflections on what helped him win these duels.
4. That he did in fact follow the Buddhist path.
5. That he trained in many arts without a teacher.
6. We know now that his art/arts were what we would call "natural." In the sense that he came to find "his" own way of doing things and in mastering one, mastered many.

It is very important for the martial artist to investigate these things in our own lives and training. Why do you love martial arts and how did it begin? Have you fought, whether in tournaments or on the street? What was the outcome? What did you learn from the experience? What is your religious or spiritual path if any? Spirituality is very important in martial arts, without it you will only understand the physical side of your art. Do you train other arts, such as painting, writing, sculpting, anything that compliments your art? Have these taught you anything about your martial training or vise versa? In our martial path it is important to truly understand why we are here and where we are headed. Without this understanding our training is nothing but a social event or sport. Not a true martial art or warrior training. Most important, why are you here? What is your ultimate goal from training your art?

In my own training I began training at a young age. I was mesmerized by the beauty of Kung Fu. I later trained for tournaments and sport. I was very unsatisfied even after winning many events. The spiritual side was missing and it cannot be experienced without "true" warrior training. This type of training involves risking life "realistic training" on occasion to further skill. "Train the body and the mind will follow." By making the body do that which the mind fears, we overcome the physical and begin to cross over to the spiritual side of our arts. This has to include various forms of meditation and an understanding and closeness with your personal choice of God.

The Ground Book

Strategy is the craft of the warrior. Commanders must enact the craft, and troopers should know this Way. There is no warrior in the world today who really understands the Way of strategy. There are various Ways. There is the Way of Salvation by the law of Buddha, the Way of Confucius governing the Way of learning, the Way of healing as a doctor, as a poet teaching the Way of Waka, tea, archery, and many arts and skills. Each man practices as he feels inclined. "Kung Fu means skill learned over time with hard work. So anyone trained in any path can be said to have Kung Fu. Master every art you choose to learn!"

It is said the warrior's is the twofold Way of pen and sword, and he should have a taste for both Ways. "Not just training to fight but other arts such as painting or others. Make the balance of Yin and Yang." Even if a man has no natural ability he can be a warrior by sticking assiduously to both divisions of the Way. Generally speaking, the Way of the warrior is resolute acceptance of death. "We live in a different world today as we no longer have fights to the death. We fight for sport or self-defense so we must obey laws or pay the price." Although not only warriors but priests, women, peasants between a few persons in a small room. I find that all men are negligent of this. There are a few men who can quickly reply to the question "What is the Way of the Warrior?" This is because they do not know in their hearts. From this we can say they do not follow the Way of the warrior. By the Way of the warrior is meant death. The Way of the warrior is death. This means choosing death whenever there is a choice between life and death. It means nothing more than this. It means to see things through, being resolved. "This reminds me of the Special Forces attitude, "never quit." "In Ninjutsu this attitude would be different. To win or escape accomplishing the mission and return home. The meaning behind the mission and taking that information back being most important. Musashi means by not fearing death we can remain calm and fight to the best of our ability. Fear causes us to hold back or freeze. The mind loses its awareness of our surroundings or situation." Sayings like "To die with your intention unrealized is to die uselessly", and so on, are from the weak Kyoto, Osaka Bushido. They are unresolved as to whether to keep to their original plan when faced with the choice of life and death. Every man wants to live. They theorize with staying alive in mind. "The man who lives on when he had failed in his intention is a coward" is a heartless definition. That to die having failed is to die uselessly is a mad point of view. This is not a shameful thing. It is the most important thing in the Way of the warrior. If you keep your spirit correct from morning to night, accustomed to the idea of death and resolved on death, and consider yourself as a dead body, thus becoming one with the Way of the warrior, you can pass through life with no possibility of failure and lowlier folk have been known to die readily in the cause of duty or out of shame, this is a different thing. The warrior is different in that studying the Way of strategy is based on overcoming men. By victory gained in crossing swords with individuals, or enjoining battle with large numbers, we can attain power and fame for ourselves or for our lord. "Kung Fu is about overcoming ourselves." This is the virtue of strategy. "Losing the fear of death comes from our spiritual path."

The Way of Strategy

In China and Japan practitioners of the Way have been known as "masters of strategy". Warriors must learn this Way. Recently there have been people getting on in the world as strategists, but they are usually just swordfencers. The attendants of the Kashima Kantori shrines'" of the province Hitachi received instruction from the gods, and made schools based on this teaching, travelling from country to country instructing men. This is the recent meaning of strategy.

In olden times strategy was listed among the Ten Abilities and Seven Arts as a beneficial practice. It was certainly an art but as beneficial practice it was not limited to sword-fencing. The true value of sword-fencing cannot be seen within the confines of sword-fencing technique.

If we look at the world we see arts for sale. Men use equipment to sell their own selves. As if with the nut and the flower, the nut has become less than the flower. In this kind of Way of strategy, both those teaching and those learning the way are concerned with coloring and showing off their technique, trying to hasten the bloom of the flower. They speak of "This Dojo" and "That Dojo".'" They are looking for profit. Someone once said "Immature strategy is the cause of grief". That was a true saying.
perform your office properly. "The servant must think earnestly of the business of his employer. Such a fellow is a splendid retainer. In this house there have been generations of splendid gentlemen and we are deeply impressed by their warm kindness ... all our ancestors. This was simply abandoning body and soul for the sake of their

lord. Moreover, our house excels in wisdom and technical skill. What a joyful thing if this can be used to advantage. Even an unadaptable man who is completely useless is a most trusted retainer if he does nothing more than think earnestly of his lord's welfare. To think only of the practical benefit of wisdom and technology is vulgar. Some men are prone to having sudden inspirations. Some men do not quickly have good ideas but arrive at the answer by slow consideration. Well, if we investigate the heart of the matter, even though people's natural abilities differ, bearing in mind the Four Oaths, when your thinking rises above concern for your own welfare, wisdom which is independent of thought appears. Whoever thinks deeply on things, even though he may carefully consider the future, will usually think around the basis of his own welfare. By the result of such evil thinking he will only perform evil acts. "Again our thoughts will control our actions. If we have a spiritual path that gives us morals to follow our actions will be accordingly." It is very difficult for most silly fellows to rise above thinking of their own welfare. "So when you embark upon something, before you start, fix your intention on the Four Oaths and put selfishness behind you. Then you cannot fail. "The Four Oaths: Never be late with respect to the Way of the warrior. "Always be on time to your training, be respectful to your Sifu or Sensei." Be useful to the lord. "This can be applied to your spiritual beliefs or perhaps to employers as well. Do whatever you do to your best ability." Be respectful to your parents. "This is very important. Parents are the ones who gave you life and you inherited your talents from them." Get beyond love and grief: exist for the good of man." "Not being selfish, sacrifice yourself for others." There are four Ways in which men pass through life: as gentlemen, farmers, artisans and merchants. The way of the farmer. Using agricultural instruments, he sees springs through to autumns with an eye on the changes of season. "An understanding of nature, either that of the universe or of mankind." Second is the Way of the merchant. The wine maker obtains his ingredients and puts them to use to make his living. The Way of the merchant is always to live by taking profit. This is the Way of the merchant. Thirdly the gentleman warrior, carrying the weaponry of his Way. The Way of the warrior is to master the virtue of his weapons. If a gentleman dislikes strategy he will not appreciate the benefit of weaponry, so must he not have a little taste for this? Fourthly the Way of the artisan. The Way of the carpenter is to become proficient in the use of his tools, first to lay his plans with a true measure and then perform his work according to plan. Thus he passes through life. These are the four Ways of the gentleman, the farmer, the artisan and the merchant.

"In Kung Fu there are four levels or paths as well. That of the warrior. That of the healer. That of the scholar. And that of the priest. These levels progress from self-protection, healing, wisdom, and finally a spiritual path."

Comparing the Way of the Carpenter to Strategy

The comparison with carpentry is through the connection with houses. Houses of the nobility, houses of warriors, the Four houses," ruin of houses, thriving of houses, the style of the house, the tradition of the house, and the name of the house. The carpenter uses a master plan of the building, and the Way of strategy is similar in that there is a plan of campaign. If you want to learn the craft of war, ponder over this book. The teacher is as a needle, the disciple is as thread. "This teaches that your teacher is the needle "guiding you the "thread" though the fabric of your art." You must practice constantly. Like the foreman carpenter, the commander must know natural rules, and the rules of the country, and the rules of houses. This is the Way of the foreman. The foreman carpenter must know the architectural theory of towers and temples, and the plans of palaces, and must employ men to raise up houses. The Way of the foreman carpenter is the same as the Way of the commander of a warrior house.

In the construction of houses, choice of woods is made. Straight un-knotted timber of good appearance is used for the revealed pillars; straight timber with small defects is used for the inner pillars. Timber of the finest appearance, even if a little weak, is used for the thresholds, lintels, doors, and sliding doors," and so on. Good strong timber, though it is gnarled and knotted, can always be used discreetly in construction. Timber which is weak or knotted throughout should be used as scaffolding, and later for firewood. The foreman carpenter allots his men work according to their ability. Floor layers, makers of sliding doors, thresholds and lintels, ceilings and so on. Those of poor ability lay the floor joist, and those of lesser ability carve wedges and do such miscellaneous work. If the foreman knows and deploys his men well the finished work will be good. The foreman should take into account the abilities and limitations of his men, circulating among them and asking nothing unreasonable. He should know their morale and spirit, and encourage them when necessary. This is the same as the principle of Four Ways strategy. "We can apply this to our training. As each man was useful in certain areas, various training methods will be also. Each method alone may not be sufficient in itself but together will give a solid foundation. These could include bag training, weights or other more traditional strength training. The use of weapons tradition or modern. Each has benefits. Flexibility training coupled with speed training or endurance. If we think of our art as the building and look to see where our own strengths and weaknesses are, we can apply these methods even if some may seem pointless at the time. We need to be as the foreman is and understand how each training method helps or hinders our art. Study each method thoroughly."

The Way of Strategy

Like a trooper, the carpenter sharpens his own tools. He carries his equipment in his tool box, and works under the direction of his foreman. He makes columns and girders with an axe, shapes floorboards and shelves with a plane, cuts fine openwork and carvings accurately, giving as excellent a finish as his skill will allow. This is the craft of carpenters. When the carpenter becomes skilled and understands measures he can become a foreman.

The carpenter's attainment is, having tools which will cut well, to make small shrines, writing shelves, tables, paper lanterns, chopping boards and pot-lids. These are the specialties of the carpenter. Things are similar for the trooper. You ought to think deeply about this. The attainment of the carpenter is that his work is not warped, that the joints are not misaligned, and that the work is truly planed so that it meets well and is not merely finished in sections. This is essential. If you want to learn this Way, deeply consider the things written in this book one at a time. You must do sufficient research. "Learning to treat our weapons with respect is a first step. Cleaning them before and after use. Learning to make them ourselves will create an even higher respect for your weapons. This will teach their strengths and weaknesses."

Outline of the Five Books of this Book of Strategy

The Way is shown in five books concerning different aspects. These are Ground, Water, Fire, Tradition (Wind)," and Void." The body of the Way of strategy from the viewpoint of my Ichi school is explained in the Ground book. It is difficult to realize the true Way just through sword-fencing. Know the smallest things and the biggest things, the shallowest things and the deepest things. "In Ninjutsu this is called "Shen Shen Shen Gan." Or the mind and eyes of God. Seeing things from a viewpoint outside of our own. As if standing outside ourselves and looking down". As if it were a straight road mapped out on the ground, the first book is called the Ground book. Second is the Water book. With water as the basis, the spirit becomes like water. Water adopts the shape of its receptacle; it is sometimes a trickle and sometimes a wild sea. Water has a clear blue color. By the clarity, things of Ichi School are shown in this book.

If you master the principles of sword-fencing, when you freely beat one man, you beat any man in the world. The spirit of defeating a man is the same for ten million men. The strategist makes small things into big things, like building a great Buddha from a one foot model. I cannot write in detail how this is done. The principle of strategy is having one thing, to know ten thousand things. Things of Ichi School are written in this the Water book. Third is the Fire book. This book is about fighting. The spirit of fire is fierce. Whether the fire is small or big; and so it is with battles. The Way of battles is the same for man to man fights and for ten thousand a side battles. You must appreciate that spirit can become big or small. What is big is easy to perceive: what is small is difficult to perceive. In short, it is difficult for large numbers of men to change position, so their movements can be easily predicted. An individual can easily change his mind, so his movements are difficult to predict. You must appreciate this. The essence of this book is that you must train day and night in order to make quick decisions. In strategy it is necessary to treat training as a part of normal life with your spirit unchanging. Thus combat in battle is described in the Fire book.

Fourthly the Wind book. This book is not concerned with My Ichi School but with other schools of strategy. By Wind I mean old traditions, present-day traditions, and family traditions of strategy. Thus I clearly explain the strategies of the world. This is tradition. It is difficult to know yourself if you do not know others. To all Ways there are side-tracks. If you study a Way daily, and your spirit diverges, you may think you are obeying a good way, but objectively it is not the true Way. If you are following the true Way and diverge a little, this will later become a large divergence. You must realize this. Other strategies have come to be thought of as mere sword-fencing, and it is not unreasonable that this should be so. The benefit of my strategy, although it includes sword-fencing, lies in a separate principle. I have explained what is commonly meant by strategy in other schools in the Tradition (Wind) book.

Fifthly, the book of the Void. By Void I mean that which has no beginning and no end. Attaining this principle means not attaining the principle. The Way of strategy is the Way of nature. When you appreciate the power of nature, knowing the rhythm of any situation, you will be able to hit the enemy naturally and strike naturally. All this is the Way of the Void. I intend to show how to follow the true Way according to nature in the book of the Void. "Mushai's five elements are worth thorough study. From a Ninjutsu standpoint we can learn:"

Earth: Rooting and physical conditioning
Water: Mental and physical flexibility. "Adapting"
Fire: Power or aggression
Wind: Acceptance and wisdom
Void: Creativity and understanding

The Name Ichi Ryu Ni To (One school-Two swords)

Warriors, both commanders and troopers, carry two swords at their belt. In olden times these were called the long sword and the sword; nowadays they are known as the sword and the companion sword. Let it suffice to say that in our land, whatever the reason, a warrior carries two swords at his belt. It is the Way of the warrior. "Nito Ichi Ryu" shows the advantage of using both swords. The spear and halberd" are weapons that are carried out of doors. Students of the Ichi School Way of strategy should train from the start with the sword and long sword in either hand. This is the truth: when you sacrifice your life, you must make fullest use of your weaponry. It is false not to do so, and to die with a weapon yet undrawn. "It is highly doubtful that Mushashi faced any challenger with two swords. The meaning of his method means using any and all ways or weapons to win. One school "The Tao" and two swords "Yin and Yang" might give you a more understanding of this method."

If you hold a sword with both hands, it is difficult to wield it freely to left and right, so my method is to carry the sword in one hand. This does not apply to large weapons such as the spear or halberd, but swords and companion swords can be carried in one hand. It is encumbering to hold a sword in both hands when you are on horseback, when running on uneven roads, on swampy ground, muddy rice fields, stony ground, or in a crowd of people. To hold the long sword in both hands is not the true Way, for if you carry a bow or spear or other arms in your left hand you have only one hand free for the long sword. However, when it is difficult to cut an enemy down with one hand, you must use both hands. It is not difficult to wield a sword in one hand; the Way to learn this is to train with two long swords, one in each hand. It will seem difficult at first, but everything is difficult at first. Bows are difficult to draw, halberds are difficult to wield; as you become accustomed to the bow so your pull will become stronger. When you become used to wielding the long sword, you will gain the power of the Way and wield the sword well.

As I will explain in the second book, the Water Book, there is no fast way of wielding the long sword. The long sword should be wielded broadly, and the companion sword closely. This is the first thing to realize. According to this Ichi School, you can win with a long weapon, and yet you can also win with a short weapon. In short, the Way of the Ichi school is the spirit of winning, whatever the weapon and whatever its size. It is better to use two swords rather than one when you are fighting a crowd and especially if you want to take a prisoner. These things cannot be explained in detail. From one thing, know ten thousand things. When you attain the Way of strategy there will not be one thing you cannot see. You must study hard.

The Benefit of the Two Characters Reading "Strategy"

Masters of the long sword are called strategists. As for the other military arts, those who master the bow are called archers, those who master the spear are called spearmen, those who master the gun are called marksmen, and those who master the halberd are called halberdiers. But we do not call masters of the Way of the long sword "longswordsmen", nor do we speak of "companion swordsmen". Because bows, guns, spears and halberds are all warriors' equipment they are certainly part of strategy. To master the virtue of the long sword is to govern the world and oneself, thus the long sword is the basis of strategy. The principle is "strategy by means of the long sword. If he attains the virtue of the long sword, one man can beat ten men. Just as one man can beat ten, so a hundred men can beat a thousand, and a thousand men can beat ten thousand. In my strategy, one man is the same as ten thousand, so this strategy is the complete
Warrior's craft.

The Way of the warrior does not include other Ways, such as Confucianism, Buddhism, certain traditions, artistic accomplishments and dancing.'" But even though these are not part of the Way, if you know the Way broadly you will see it in everything. Men must polish their particular Way. "Here I have to disagree with Musashi. As my teacher used to say, "Knowledge of other arts is like spokes in a wheel. The more spokes, the stronger the wheel." I believe learning any and all arts can benefit our training. In addition to Ninja training being able to perform other things such as occupations allows us to disguise ourselves in plain sight."

The Benefit of Weapons in Strategy

There is a time and a place for use of weapons. The best use of the companion sword is in a confined space, or when you are engaged closely with an opponent. The long sword can be used effectively in all situations. The halberd is inferior to the spear on the battlefield. With the spear you can take the initiative; the halberd is defensive. In the hands of one of two men of equal ability, the spear gives a little extra strength. Spear and halberd both have their uses, but neither is very beneficial in confined spaces. They cannot be used for taking a prisoner. They are essentially weapons for the field. Anyway, if you learn "indoor" techniques, you will think narrowly and forget the true Way. Thus you will have difficulty in actual encounters. The bow is tactically strong at the commencement of battle, especially battles on a moor, as it is possible to shoot quickly from among the spearmen. However, it is unsatisfactory in sieges, or when the enemy is more than forty yards away. For this reason there are nowadays few traditional schools of archery. There is little use nowadays for this kind of skill.

From inside fortifications, the gun has no equal among weapons. It is the supreme weapon on the field before the ranks clash, but once swords are crossed the gun becomes useless. "In today's world this statement is more true than ever. Guns are the most powerful weapon a non-military person can acquire. But each will again have its strength and weaknesses. The rifle for maximum range. Keeping us safe from the enemies attack. The shotgun, less accurate and shorter range but packs a powerful punch at close range. The perfect weapon for multiple opponents. Last the handgun. A great weapon for close range but is a disadvantage once grappling begins". One of the virtues of the bow is that you can see the arrows in flight and correct your aim accordingly, whereas gunshot cannot be seen. You must appreciate the importance of this. "The bow is still an effective weapon. Great for when silence is a must. The crossbow is perfect for this situation."

Just as a horse must have endurance and no defects, so it is with weapons. Horses should walk strongly, and swords and companion swords should cut strongly. Spears and halberds must stand up to heavy use: bows and guns must be sturdy. Weapons should be hardy rather than decorative. "Tournament vs. Traditional." You should not have a favorite weapon. To become overfamiliar with one weapon is as much a fault as not knowing it sufficiently well. You should not copy others, but use weapons which you can handle properly. It is bad for commanders and troops to have likes and dislikes. These are things you must learn thoroughly. "The Shaolin monks would learn the 18 weapons in their training. This allowed them to be able to fight against any of them in combat. By knowing how to use each there would be no excuse not to use a weapon dropped by someone in battle. Although we all will have our favorite weapon, we should learn to use all of them. Different weapons are useful at different ranges. In modern terms we might think of the rifle for long range. If the enemy comes too close we could switch to our handgun. When the opponent closes the gap, our knife might then be the best weapon for combat. Traditional might be staff or whip chain. Then midrange nunchaku, escrima sticks etc., then lastly for close range daggers, Kubota sometimes called Yawara or thunderbolt stick. Our empty hand techniques can be broken down as well. Skip in or leaping forward kicks covering distance. Known mostly in Dragon, Leopard, and Crane styles. Midrange would be standing in place kicking. Then punching, followed then by knees and elbows. Lastly the closest range would be grappling."

Timing in Strategy

There is timing in everything. Timing in strategy cannot be mastered without a great deal of practice. Timing is important in dancing and pipe or string music, for they are in rhythm only if timing is good. Timing and rhythm are also involved in the military arts, shooting bows and guns, and riding horses. In all skills and abilities there is timing. There is also timing in the Void. There is timing in the whole life of the warrior, in his thriving and declining, in his harmony and discord. Similarly, there is timing in the Way of the merchant, in the rise and fall of capital. All things entail rising and falling timing. You must be able to discern this. In strategy there are various timing considerations. From the outset you must know the applicable timing and the inapplicable timing, and from among the large and small things and the fast and slow timings find the relevant timing, first seeing the distance timing and the background timing. This is the main thing in strategy. It is especially important to know the background timing; otherwise your strategy will become uncertain.

You win in battles with the timing in the Void born of the timing of cunning by knowing the enemies' timing, and this using a timing which the enemy does not expect. "This applies to the fives ways of fighting. The five elements teach us timing in combat that will of course flow from one element to the other. Earth will be used by those who can endure punishment and are very confident in their ability. Water is used for those who are agile and have good footwork. These fighters can adapt to their opponent waiting for the right moment to counter attack. Fire is used against a timid opponent or when they are injured. Here aggression is the key. Wind is for the very skilled. Their movements will be effortless and move around attacks like a leaf floating on the wind. Lastly is the Void. Fighting from the Void element we outthink our opponent. Using methods perhaps not normally thought of as martial. Feigning weakness or fear, or perhaps using escape methods. The Void is also where all the other four methods come from. So fighting from the Void is moving from one method to the other as needed in order to win."

All the five books are chiefly concerned with timing. You must train sufficiently to appreciate all this. If you practice day and night in the above Ichi school strategy, your spirit will naturally broaden. Thus is large scale strategy and the strategy of hand to hand combat propagated in the world. This is recorded for the first time in the five books of Ground, Water, Fire, Tradition (Wind), and Void. This is the Way for men who want to learn my Strategy:

Do not think dishonestly.

The Way is in training.

Become acquainted with every art.

Know the Ways of all professions.

Distinguish between gain and loss in worldly matters.

Develop intuitive judgment and understanding for everything.

Perceive those things which cannot be seen.

Pay attention even to trifles.

Do nothing which is of no use. *"Get rid of the TV and train!"*

It is important to start by setting these broad principles in your heart, and train in the Way of strategy. If you do not look at things on a large scale it will be difficult for you to master strategy. If you learn and attain this strategy you will never lose even to twenty or thirty enemies. More than anything to start with you must set your heart on strategy and earnestly stick to the Way. You will come to be able to actually beat men in fights, and to be able to win with your eye. Also by training you will be able to freely control your own body, conquer men with your body, and with sufficient training you will be able to beat ten men with your spirit. When you have reached this point, will it not mean that you are invincible?

Moreover, in large scale strategy the superior man will manage many subordinates dexterously, bear himself correctly, govern the country and foster the people, thus preserving the ruler's discipline. If there is a Way involving the spirit of not being defeated, to help oneself and gain honor, it is the Way of strategy.

The second year of Shoho (1645), the fifth month, the twelfth day.

Teruo Magonojo" SHINMEN MUSASHI

The Water Book

The spirit of the Ni Ten Ichi School of strategy is based on water, and this Water Book explains methods of victory as the long-sword form of the Ichi School. Language does not extend to explaining the Way in detail, but it can be grasped intuitively. Study this book; read a word then ponder on it. If you interpret the meaning loosely you will mistake the Way.

The principles of strategy are written down here in terms of single combat, but you must think broadly so that you attain an understanding for ten-thousand-a-side battles. Strategy is different from other things in that if you mistake the Way even a little you will become bewildered and fall into bad ways. "Your form training needs to be approached the same way. Take each move separately, and investigate offensively and defensively."

If you merely read this book you will not reach the Way of strategy. Absorb the things written in this book. Do not just read, memorize or imitate, but so that you realize the principle from within your own heart study hard to absorb these things into your body.

Spiritual Bearing in Strategy

In strategy your spiritual bearing must not be any different from normal. Both in fighting and in everyday life you should be determined though calm. Meet the situation without tenseness yet not recklessly, your spirit settled yet unbiased. Even when your spirit is calm do not let your body relax, and when your body is relaxed do not let your spirit slacken. Do not let your spirit be influenced by your body, or your body influenced by your spirit. Be neither insufficiently spirited nor over spirited. An elevated spirit is weak and a low spirit is weak. Do not let the enemy see your spirit. "This is called the fighter's awareness." Develop the five senses and constantly be aware of your surroundings. Ready to defend yourself at any time." Here meditations such as Zazen or for Chinese arts using the more popular nei gongs are useful. The horse stance was used by the Shaolin monks as a way to train meditation under very painful conditions. This training teaches you to relax and be aware even in dangerous situations."

Small people must be completely familiar with the spirit of large people, and large people must be familiar with the spirit of small people. Whatever your size, do not be misled by the reactions of your own body. With your spirit open and unconstricted, look at things from a high point of view. You must cultivate your wisdom and spirit. Polish your wisdom: learn public justice, distinguish between good and evil, study the Ways of different arts one by one. When you cannot be deceived by men you will have realized the wisdom of strategy. "Knowing how others fight is a key strength. What are the strengths of larger opponents? Smaller ones? Grapplers or boxers? Even kickers."

The wisdom of strategy is different from other things. On the battlefield, even when you are hard-pressed, you should ceaselessly research the principles of strategy so that you can develop a steady spirit.

Stance in Strategy

Adopt a stance with the head erect, neither hanging down, nor looking up, nor twisted. Your forehead and the space between your eyes should not be wrinkled. Do not roll your eyes nor allow them to blink, but slightly narrow them. With your features composed, keep the line of your nose straight with a feeling of slightly flaring your nostrils. Hold the line of the rear of the neck straight: instill vigor into your hairline, and in the same way from the shoulders down through your entire body. Lower both shoulders and, without the buttocks jutting out, put strength into your legs from the knees to the tops of your toes. Brace your abdomen so that you do not bend at the hips. Wedge your companion sword in your belt against your abdomen, so that your belt is not slack — this is called "wedging in". In all forms of strategy, it is necessary to maintain the combat stance in everyday life and to make your everyday stance your combat stance. You must research this well. "The head position Mushashi teaches here is used to activate the "reptilian" brain. A mindset that allows the human being to act like an animal. Cold hearted, without anger, under control and deadly."

The Gaze in Strategy

The gaze should be large and broad. This is the two-fold gaze "Perception and Sight". Perception is strong and sight weak. In strategy it is important to see distant things as if they were close and to take a distanced view of close things. It is important in strategy to know the enemy's sword and not to be distracted by insignificant movements of his sword. You must study this. The gaze is the same for single combat and for large-scale combat.

It is necessary in strategy to be able to look to both sides without moving the eyeballs. You cannot master this ability quickly. Learn what is written here: use this gaze in everyday life and do not vary it whatever happens. "This is the gaze used in Kung Fu during most standing chi kungs. Looking off into the distance while being aware of areas to the left and right. The eyes should be relaxed, almost as if falling asleep. Sometimes called Tiger's eye."

Holding the Long Sword

Grip the long sword with a rather floating feeling in your thumb and forefinger, with the middle finger neither tight nor slack, and with the last two fingers tight. It is bad to have play in your hands. When you take up a sword, you must feel intent on cutting the enemy. As you cut an enemy you must not change your grip, and your hands must not "cower". When you dash the enemy's sword aside, or ward it off, or force it down, you must slightly change the feeling in your thumb and forefinger. Above all, you must be intent on cutting the enemy in the way you grip the sword. The grip for combat and for sword-testing is the same. There is no such thing as a "man-cutting grip". "Train all skills as if to kill. Not to play or score points. The point of combat is to win, not play." "Do not spar, fight!"

Generally, I dislike fixedness in both long swords and hands. Fixedness means a dead hand. Pliability is a living hand. You must bear this in mind.

Footwork

With the tips of your toes somewhat floating, tread firmly with your heels. Whether you move fast or slow, with large or small steps, your feet must always move as in normal walking. I dislike the three walking methods known as "jumping-foot", "floating-foot" and "fixed-steps". So-called "Yin-Yang foot" is important to the Way. Yin-Yang foot means not moving only one foot. It means moving your feet left-right and right-left when cutting, withdrawing, or warding off a cut. You should not move one foot preferentially. "Yin Yang foot very similar to the metal or double metal step in Hsing I."

The Five Attitudes

The five attitudes are: Upper, Middle, Lower, Right Side, and Left Side. These are the five. Although attitude has these five dimensions, the one purpose of all of them is to cut the enemy. There are none but these five attitudes. Whatever attitude you are in, do not be conscious of making the attitude; think only of cutting. Your attitude should be large or small according to the situation. Upper, Lower and Middle attitudes are decisive. Left Side and Right Side attitudes are fluid. Left and Right attitudes should be used if there is an obstruction overhead or to one side. The decision to use Left or Right depends on the place. "Using Chinese thought this would be Heaven,

Man, and Earth levels. Left and right would be Yin left and Yang right. During any attack or defense you will be in one of these. Without a weapon the lead hand guard position will be high or Heaven, middle or Man, or Earth which is low. You may also be in two at once such as in Crane style posture where one is held high and one low. The front knee raised to complete the Heaven, Man, and Earth guarding positions. One should think of the three guards not only to the front but the left and right as well as to the rear. Thinking of being not stationary but moving fluidly in a 360 degree pattern around you. Any low line attacks should always be defended with the shins or knees, leaving the hands free to protect man and heaven levels. Internal martial artists may recognize this in the three tan tians. Yin tang, tan jung, and tan tien."

The essence of the Way is this. To understand attitude you must thoroughly understand the Middle attitude. The Middle attitude is the heart of the attitudes. If we look at strategy on a broad scale, the Middle attitude is the seat of the commander, with the other four attitudes following the commander. You must appreciate this. "Study your own forms from your art. Notice where the guards or blocks are in each move. Using the above positions what areas are they covering? Notice how one may be guarding or attacking high and blocking low to the rear. Study each move and apply the positions above to each one."

The Way of the Long Sword

Knowing the Way of the long sword means we can wield with two fingers the sword that we usually carry. If we know the path of the sword well, we can wield it easily.

If you try to wield the long sword quickly you will mistake the Way. To wield the long sword well you must wield it calmly. If you try to wield it quickly, like a folding fan"" or a short sword, you will err by using "short sword chopping". You cannot cut a man with a long sword using this method. When you have cut downwards with the long sword, lift it straight upwards, when you cut sideways, return the sword along a sideways path. Return the sword in a reasonable way, always stretching the elbows broadly. Wield the sword strongly. This is the Way of the long sword.

If you learn to use the five approaches of my strategy, you will be able to wield a sword well. You must train constantly.

The Five Approaches

The first approach is the Middle attitude. Confront the enemy with the point of your sword against his face. When he attacks, dash his sword to the right and "ride" it. Or, when the enemy attacks, deflect the point of his sword by hitting downwards, keep your long sword where it is, and as the enemy renews the attack cut his arms from below. This is the first method.

The five approaches are this kind of thing. You must train repeatedly using a long sword in order to learn them. When you master my Way of the long sword, you will be able to control any attack the enemy makes. I assure you, there are no attitudes other than the five attitudes of the long sword of NiTo.

In the second approach with the long sword, from the Upper attitude cut the enemy just as he attacks. If the enemy evades the cut, keep your sword where it is and, scooping from below, cut him as he renews the attack. It is possible to repeat the cut from here. In this method there are various changes in timing and spirit. You will be able to understand this by training in the Ichi School. You will always win with the five long sword methods. You must train repeatedly.

In the third approach, adopt the Lower attitude, anticipating scooping up. When the enemy attacks, hit his hands from below. As you do so, he may try to hit your sword down. If this is the case, cut his upper arm(s) horizontally with a feeling of "crossing". This means that from the Lower attitudes you hit the enemy at the instant that he attacks. You will encounter this method often, both as a beginner and in later strategy. You must train holding a long sword.

In this fourth approach, adopt the Left Side attitude. As the enemy attacks, hit his hands from below. If as you hit his hands he attempts to dash down your sword, with the feeling of hitting his hands, parry the path of his long sword and cut across from above your shoulder. This is the Way of the long sword. Through this method you win by parrying the line of the enemy's attack. You must study this.

In the fifth approach, the sword is in the Right Side attitude. In accordance with the enemy's attack, cross your sword from below at the side to the Upper attitude. Then cut straight from above. This method is essential for knowing the Way of the long sword well. If you can use this method, you can freely wield a heavy long sword.

I cannot describe in detail how to use these five approaches. You must become well acquainted with my "in harmony with the long sword" Way, learn large-scale timing, understand the enemy's long sword, and become used to the five approaches from the outset. You will always win by using these five methods, with various timing considerations discerning the enemy's spirit. You must consider all this carefully. "The five attitudes or stances, give us a foundation to launch attacks or defend. Each style will have its own postures with various hand positions. Using the above description by Musashi take each posture with Heaven, Earth, and Man levels in mind and train for attack and counter attacks. Keeping in mind that there are no other than high, middle, low, left, and right guards. There can also high left or right. Low left or right. Investigate the meaning of your stances and see why they were created by the masters who passed on their wisdom. The Chinese masters of old understood this long before Mushashi because it is a "universal" truth."

The "Attitude-No-Attitude" Teaching

"Attitude No-Attitude" means that there is no need for what are known as long sword attitudes. Even so, attitudes exist as the five ways of holding the long sword. However you hold the sword it must be in such a way that it is easy to cut the enemy well, in accordance with the situation, the place, and your relation to the enemy. From the Upper attitude as your spirit lessens you can adopt the Middle attitude, and from the Middle attitude you can raise the sword a little in your technique and adopt the Upper attitude. From the Lower attitude you can raise the sword a little and adopt the Middle attitudes as the occasion demands. According to the situation, if you turn your sword from either the Left Side or Right Side attitude towards the center, the Middle or the Lower attitude results. The principle of this is called "Existing Attitude — Non-existing Attitude".

The primary thing when you take a sword in your hands is your intention to cut the enemy, whatever the means. Whenever you parry, hit, spring, strike or touch the enemy's cutting sword, you must cut the enemy in the same movement. It is essential to attain this. If you think only of hitting, springing, striking or touching the enemy, you will not be able actually to cut him. More than anything, you must be thinking of carrying your movement through to cutting him. You must thoroughly research this. Attitude in strategy on a larger scale is called "Battle Array". Such attitudes are all for winning battles. Fixed formation is bad. Study this well. "Watching Bruce Lee in Enter the dragon, we can see the constant moving hands and feet. Bruce was not giving the opponent anything to go on for attack."

To Hit the Enemy "In One Timing"

"In One Timing" means, when you have closed with the enemy, to hit him as quickly and directly as possible, without moving your body or settling your spirit, while you see that he is still undecided. The timing of hitting before the enemy decides to withdraw, break or hit, is this "In One Timing". You must train to achieve this timing, to be able to hit in the timing of an instant. "Train to hit the opponent immediately after he has blocked an attack." While he is still off balance." The "Abdomen Timing of Two" When you attack and the enemy quickly retreats, as you see him tense you must feint a cut. Then, as he relaxes, follow up and hit him. This is the "Abdomen Timing of Two". It is very difficult to attain this merely by reading this book, but you will soon understand with a little instruction. "Sometimes called stutter hitting. Faking a strike slowly to get a reaction then a swift powerful attack. This uses a broken rhythm."

No Design, No Conception

In this method, when the enemy attacks and you decide to attack, hit with your body, and hit with your spirit, and hit from the Void with your hands, accelerating strongly. This is the "No Design, No Conception" cut. This is the most important method of hitting. It is often used. You must train hard to understand it. "In Chinese we would say hit with Mind, Body, and Spirit. Where thought and action are one."

The Flowing Water Cut

The "Flowing Water Cut" is used when you are struggling blade to blade with the enemy. When he breaks and quickly withdraws trying to spring with his long sword, expand your body and spirit and cut him as slowly as possible with your long sword, following your body like stagnant water. You can cut with certainty if you learn this. You must discern the enemy's grade.

Continuous Cut

When you attack and the enemy also attacks and your swords spring together, in one action cut his head, hands and legs. When you cut several places with one sweep of the long sword, it is the "Continuous Cut". You must practice this cut; it is often used. With detailed practice you should be able to understand it. "This is used extensively in the Escrima and Penjak Silat arts. For example hitting with the hips followed by shoulder, elbows, forearms, fist, and lastly the fingertips."

The Fire and Stones Cut

The Fires and Stones Cut means that when the enemy's long sword and your long sword clash together you cut as strongly as possible without raising the sword even a little. This means cutting quickly with the hands, body and legs all three cutting strongly. If you train well enough you will be able to strike strongly. "Practice hitting at zero distance using the whole body and intention. Called Fajing in Tai Chi Chuan."

The Red Leaves Cut

The Red Leaves Cut means knocking down the enemy's long sword. The spirit should be getting control of his sword. When the enemy is in a long sword attitude in front of you and intent on cutting, hitting and parrying, you strongly hit the enemy's sword with the Fire and Stones Cut, perhaps in the design of the "No Design, No

Conception" Cut. If you then beat down the point of his sword with a sticky feeling, he will necessarily drop the sword. If you practice this cut it becomes easy to make the enemy drop his sword. You must train repetitively. "Wing chun is a very good example of this. Parrying down the lead or attacking hand while "trapping" it in place."

The Body in Place of the Long Sword

Also "the long sword in place of the body". Usually we move the body and the sword at the same time to cut the enemy. However, according to the enemy's cutting method, you can dash against him with your body first and afterwards cut with the sword. If his body is immoveable, you can cut first with the long sword, but generally you hit first with the body and then cut with the long sword. You must research this well and practice hitting. "An empty hand example would be from Tai Chi Chuan. Using the shoulder strike at close range to know the opponent back and whipping the fingers to the eyes as he falls backward."

Cut and Slash

To cut and slash are two different things. Cutting, whatever form of cutting it is, is decisive, with a resolute spirit. Slashing is nothing more than touching the enemy. Even if you slash strongly, and even if the enemy dies instantly, it is slashing. When you cut, your spirit is resolved. You must appreciate this. If you first slash the enemy's hands or legs, you must then cut strongly. Slashing is in spirit the same as touching. When you realize this, they become indistinguishable. Learn this well. "Think of hitting and killing with one hit, not to intimidate or hurt."

Chinese Monkey's Body

The Chinese Monkey's Body is the spirit of not stretching out your arms. The spirit is to get in quickly, without in the least extending your arms, before the enemy cuts. If you are intent upon not stretching out your arms you are effectively far away, the spirit is to go in with your whole body. When you come to within arm's reach it becomes easy to move your body in. You must research this well. "Monkey Kung Fu is great at using this. Keeping the hands in guard close to the body keeps the opponent from trapping them. Sometimes feigning weakness by slightly turning the back toward the opponent. Then suddenly springing in to attack or spinning the opposite direction as in spinning back fist high or low."

Glue and Lacquer Emulsion Body

The spirit of "Glue and Lacquer Emulsion Body" is to stick to the enemy and not separate from him. When you approach the enemy, stick firmly with your head, body and legs. People tend to advance their head and legs quickly, but their body lags behind. You should stick firmly so that there is not the slightest gap between the enemy's body and your body. You must consider this carefully. "Used in grappling but also sticky body, a form of sticky hands from Tai Chi Chuan."

To Strive for Height

By "to strive for height" is meant, when you close with the enemy, to strive with him for superior height without cringing. Stretch your legs, stretch your hips, and stretch your neck face to face with him. When you think you have won, and you are the higher, thrust in strongly. You must learn this. "In empty hand martial arts if the opponent is taller we can reach the higher ground by attacking the knees bringing the head down to our reach."

To Apply Stickiness

When the enemy attacks and you also attack with the long sword, you should go in with a sticky feeling and fix your long sword against the enemy's as you receive his cut. The Spirit of stickiness is not hitting very strongly, but hitting so that the long swords do not separate easily. It is best to approach as calmly as possible when hitting the enemy's long sword with stickiness. The difference between "Stickiness" and "Entanglement" is that stickiness is firm and entanglement is weak. You must appreciate this. "Practice sticky hands in Tai Chi or Wing Chun."

The Body Strike

The Body Strike means to approach the enemy through a gap in his guard. The spirit is to strike him with your body. Turn your face a little aside and strike the enemy's breast with your left shoulder thrust out. Approach with a spirit of bouncing the enemy away, striking as strongly as possible in time with your breathing. If you achieve this method of closing with the enemy, you will be able to knock him ten or twenty feet away. It is possible to strike the enemy until he is dead. Train well. "An awesome technique known to Tai chi practice, known as "Kao." Practice this technique by pushing the heavy bag away from you and striking with your shoulder as it swings back into range. This will also teach timing and distance. A more advanced method is hitting trees until you can make the leaves shake. Do at your own risk."

Three Ways to Parry His Attack

There are three methods to parry a cut: First, by dashing the enemy's long sword to your right, as if thrusting at his eyes when he makes an attack. Or, to parry by thrusting the enemy's long sword towards his right eye with the feeling of snipping his neck. Or, when you have a short "long sword", without worrying about parrying the enemy's long sword, to close with him quickly, thrusting at his face with your left hand. These are the three ways of parrying. You must bear in mind that you can always clench your left hand and thrust at the enemy's face with your fist. For this it is necessary to train well. "This is trained in Wing Chun and is called "Bridging." The attacking hand actually blocks and strikes in the same movement."

To Stab at the Face

To stab at the face means, when you are in confrontation with the enemy, that your spirit is intent on stabbing at his face, following the line of the blades with the point of your long sword. If you are intent on stabbing at his face, his face and body will become rideable. When the enemy becomes rideable, there are various opportunities for winning. You must concentrate on this. When fighting and the enemy's body becomes as if rideable, you can win quickly, so you ought not to forget to stab at the face. You must pursue the value of this technique through training. "An effective and sometimes fight ending strike. Train attacks to the eyes using finger jabs, whipping strikes "Tai chi and Crane" as well as finger flicks."

To Stab at the Heart

To stab at the heart means, when fighting and there are obstructions above or to the sides, and whenever it is difficult to cut, to thrust at the enemy. You must stab the enemy's breast without letting the point of your long sword waver, showing the enemy the ridge of the blade square-on, and with the spirit of deflecting his long sword. The spirit of this principle is often useful when we become tired or for some reason our long sword will not cut. You must understand the application of this method. "Again excellent technique of attacking the centerline in Wing Chun."

To Scold "Tut-TUT!"

"Scold" means that, when the enemy tries to counter-cut as you attack, you counter-cut again from below as if thrusting at him, trying to hold him down. With very quick timing you cut, scolding the enemy. Thrust up, "Tut!", and cut "TUT!" This timing is encountered time and time again in exchanges of blows. The way to scold Tut-TUT is to time the cut simultaneously with raising your long sword as if to thrust the enemy. You must learn this through repetitive practice. "Used a lot in Mantis or Crane styles. Using a rising beak block followed by immediate counter attack."

The Smacking Parry

By "smacking parry" is meant that when you clash swords with the enemy, you meet his attacking cut on your long sword with a tee-dum, tee-dum rhythm, smacking his sword and cutting him. The spirit of the smacking parry is not parrying, or smacking strongly, but smacking the enemy's long sword in accordance with his attacking cut, primarily intent on quickly cutting him. If you understand the timing of smacking, however hard your long swords clash together, your sword point will not be knocked back even a little. You must research sufficiently to realize this. "The use of Pak Sao in Wing chung."

There are Many Enemies

"There are many enemies'" applies when you are fighting one against many. Draw both sword and companion sword and assume a wide-stretched left and right attitude. The spirit is to chase the enemies around from side to side, even though they come from all four directions. Observe their attacking order, and go to meet first those who attack first. Sweep your eyes around broadly, carefully examining the attacking order, and cut left and right alternately with your swords. Waiting is bad. Always quickly reassume your attitudes to both sides, cut the enemies down as they advance, crushing them in the direction from which they attack. Whatever you do, you must drive the enemy together, as if tying a line of fishes, and when they are seen to be piled up, cut them down strongly without giving them room to move. "I mentioned this earlier. Keep moving using the three dimensional guarding attitude. Move around attackers as you strike and use them as barriers from other attacker. They get in each other's way. Bagau teaches to fight up to eight attackers at a time. The number is because of the eight angles. North,

South, East, and West. Plus the four corners. There are no other openings."

The Advantage When Coming to Blows

You can know how to win through strategy with the long sword, but it cannot be clearly explained in writing. You must practice diligently in order to understand how to win. Oral tradition 'The true Way of strategy is revealed in the long sword." As in most traditional martial arts especially Kung Fu, much information is not given out publicly or written in books. It is only handed down orally to selected students."

One Cut

You can win with certainty with the spirit of "one cut". It is difficult to attain this if you do not learn strategy well. If you train well in this Way, strategy will come from your heart and you will be able to win at will. You must train diligently. "Train to win with one strike.|

Direct Communication

The spirit of "Direct Communication" is how the true Way of the NiTo Ichi School is received and handed down.

Oral tradition: "Teach your body strategy."

Recorded in the above book is an outline of Ichi school sword fighting. To learn how to win with the long sword in strategy, first learn the five approaches and the five attitudes, and absorb the Way of the long sword naturally in your body. You must understand spirit and timing, handle the long sword naturally, and move body and legs in harmony with your spirit. Whether beating one man or two, you will then know values in strategy.

Study the contents of this book, taking one item at a time, and through fighting with enemies you will gradually come to know the principle of the Way. Deliberately, with a patient spirit, absorb the virtue of all this, from time to time raising your hand in combat. Maintain this spirit whenever you cross swords with an enemy. Step by step walk the thousand-mile road.

Study strategy over the years and achieve the spirit of the warrior. Today is victory over yourself of yesterday; tomorrow is your victory over lesser men. Next, in order to beat more skillful men, train according to this book, not allowing your heart to be swayed along a side-track. Even if you kill an enemy, if it is not based on what you have learned it is not the true Way. If you attain this Way of victory, then you will be able to beat several tens of men. What remains is sword-fighting ability, which you can attain in battles and duels.

The Second Year of Shoho, the twelfth day of the fifth month (1645) Teruo Magonojo SHINMEN MUSAS

The Fire Book

In this the Fire Book of the NiTo Ichi School of strategy I describe fighting as fire. In the first place, people think narrowly about the benefit of strategy. By using only their fingertips, they only know the benefit of three of the five inches of the wrist. They let a contest be decided, as with the folding fan, merely by the span of their forearms. They specialize in the small matter of dexterity, learning such trifles as hand and leg movements with the bamboo practice sword.

In my strategy, the training for killing enemies is by way of many contests, fighting for survival, discovering the meaning of life and death, learning the Way of the sword, judging the strength of attacks and understanding the Way of the "edge and ridge" of the sword. You cannot profit from small techniques particularly when full armor is worn. "Today's combat is much different. In Kung Fu there are many small effective strikes." My Way of strategy is the sure method to win when fighting for your life one man against five or ten. There is nothing wrong with the principle "one man can beat ten, so a thousand men can beat ten thousand". You must research this. Of course you cannot assemble a thousand or ten thousand men for everyday training. But you can become a master of strategy by training alone with a sword, so that you can understand the enemy's strategies, his strength and resources, and come to appreciate how to apply strategy to beat ten thousand enemies.

Any man who wants to master the essence of my strategy must research diligently, training morning and evening. Thus can he polish his skill, become free from self, and realize extraordinary ability. He will come to posess miraculous power. This is the practical result of strategy.

Depending on the Place Examine your environment

Stand in the sun; that is, take up an attitude with the sun behind you. If the situation does not allow this, you must try to keep the sun on your right side. In buildings, you must stand with the entrance behind you or to your right. Make sure that your rear is unobstructed, and that there is free space on your left, your right side being occupied with your sword attitude. At night, if the enemy can be seen, keep the fire behind you and the entrance to your right, and otherwise take up your attitude as above. You must look down on the enemy, and take up your attitude on slightly higher places. When the fight comes, always endeavor to chase the enemy around to your left side. "Musashi says this as the sword is in the right hand. But this can be applied to attackers who are in left or right leads. Move away from the rear or power hand. Circling footwork. Chase him towards awkward places, and try to keep him with his back to awkward places. When the enemy gets into an inconvenient position, do not let him look around, but conscientiously chase him around and pin him down. In houses, chase the enemy into the thresholds, lintels, doors, verandas, pillars, and so on, again not letting him see his situation. "Can be applied to using sweeps, trips, and stepping on the foot holding it in place. When entering buildings always check exits and entrances for escape."

Always chase the enemy into bad footholds, obstacles at the side, and so on, using the virtues of the place to establish predominant positions from which to fight. You must research and train diligently in this.

The Three Methods to Forestall the Enemy

The first is to forestall him by attacking. This is called Ken No Sen (to set him up). Another method is to forestall him as he attacks. This is called Tai No Sen (to wait for the initiative). The other method is when you and the enemy attack together. This is called Tai Tai No Sen (to accompany him and forestall him).

There are no methods of taking the lead other than these three. Because you can win quickly by taking the lead, it is one of the most important things in strategy. There are several things involved in taking the lead. You must make the best of the situation, see through the enemy's spirit so that you grasp his strategy and defeat him. It is impossible to write about this in detail.

The First-Ken No Sen

When you decide to attack, keep calm and dash in quickly, forestalling the enemy. Or you can advance seemingly strongly but with a reserved spirit, forestalling him with the reserve. Alternately, advance with as strong a spirit as possible, and when you reach the enemy move with your feet a little quicker than normal, unsettling him and overwhelming him sharply. Or, with your spirit calm, attack with a feeling of constantly crushing the enemy, from first to last. The spirit is to win in the depths of the enemy. These are all Ken No Sen.

The Second-Tai No Sen

When the enemy attacks, remain undisturbed but feign weakness. As the enemy reaches you, suddenly move away indicating that you intend to jump aside, then dash in attacking strongly as soon as you see the enemy relax. This is one way or, as the enemy attacks, attacks more strongly, taking advantage of the resulting disorder in his timing to win. This is the Tai No Sen Principle.

The Third-Tai Tai No Sen

When the enemy makes a quick attack, you must attack strongly and calmly, aim for his weak point as he draws near, and strongly defeat him. Or, if the enemy attacks calmly, you must observe his movement and, with your body rather floating, join in with his movements as he draws near. Move quickly and cut him strongly. This is Tai Tai No Sen These things cannot be clearly explained in words. You must research what is written here. In these three ways of forestalling, you must judge the situation. This does not mean that you always attack first; but if the enemy attacks first you can lead him around. In strategy, you have effectively won when you forestall the enemy, so you must train well to attain this.

To Hold Down a Pillow

"To hold down a Pillow" means not allowing the enemy's head to rise. "Called Tiger plays with ball in Kung Fu." Controlling the head controls the body. The neck contains arteries and the windpipe that supply oxygen and blood to the brain. Controlling this area is vital in knockouts, chokes or killing quickly."

In contests of strategy it is bad to be led about by the enemy. You must always be able to lead the enemy about. Obviously the enemy will also be thinking of doing this, but he cannot forestall you if you do not allow him to come out. In strategy, you must stop the enemy as he attempts to cut; you must push down his thrust, and throw off his hold when he tries to grapple. This is the meaning of "to hold down a pillow". When you have grasped this principle, whatever the enemy tries to bring about in the fight you will see in advance and suppress it. The spirit is to check his attack at the syllable "at . . ." when he jumps check his advance at the syllable "ju . . .", and check his cut at "cu . . ."

The important thing in strategy is to suppress the enemy's useful actions but allow his useless actions. However, doing this alone is defensive. First, you must act according to the Way, suppress the enemy's techniques, foiling his plans, and thence command him directly. When you can do this you will be a master of strategy. You must train well and research "holding down a pillow".

Crossing at a Ford

"Crossing at a ford" means, for example, crossing the sea at a strait, or crossing over a hundred miles of broad sea at a crossing place. I believe this "crossing at a ford" occurs often in a man's lifetime. It means setting sail even though your friends stay in harbor, knowing the route, knowing the soundness of your ship and the favor of the day. When all the conditions are met, and there is perhaps a favorable wind, or a tailwind, then set sail. If the wind changes within a few miles of your destination, you must row across the remaining distance without sail. If you attain this spirit, it applies to everyday life. You must always think of crossing at a ford.

In strategy also it is important to "cross at a ford". Discern the enemy's capability and, knowing your own strong points, "cross the ford" at the advantageous place, as a good captain crosses a sea route. If you succeed in crossing at the best place, you may take your ease. To cross at a ford means to attack the enemy's weak point, and to put yourself in an advantageous position. This is how to win in large-scale strategy. The spirit of crossing at a ford is necessary in both large — and small-scale strategy. You must research this well. "A version of counterattacking. Or after a using a few strikes to feel out the opponent, attack his weakness."

To Know the Times

"To know the times" means to know the enemy's disposition in battle. Is it flourishing or waning? By observing the spirit of the enemy's men and getting the best position, you can work out the enemy's disposition and move your men accordingly. You can win through this principle of strategy, fighting from a position of advantage. When in a duel, you must forestall the enemy and attack when you have first recognized his school of strategy, perceived his quality and his strong and weak points. Attack in an unsuspected manner, knowing his meter and modulation and the appropriate timing. Knowing the times means, if your ability is high, seeing right into things. If you are thoroughly conversant with strategy, you will recognize the enemy's intentions and thus have many opportunities to win. You must sufficiently study this.

To Tread Down the Sword

"To tread down the sword" is a principle often used in strategy. First, in large-scale strategy, when the enemy first discharges bows and guns and then attacks, it is difficult for us to attack if we are busy loading powder into our guns or notching our arrows. The spirit is to attack quickly while the enemy is still shooting with bows or guns. The spirit is to win by "treading down" as we receive the enemy's attack. "Attack while the opponent is off balance, trying to regain footing, or catching his breath."

In single combat, we cannot get a decisive victory by cutting, with a "tee-dum tee- dum" feeling, in the wake of the enemy's attacking long sword. We must defeat him at the start of his attack, in the spirit of treading him down with the feet, so that he cannot rise again to the attack.

"Treading" does not simply mean treading with the feet. Tread with the body, tread with the spirit, and, of course, tread and cut with the long sword. You must achieve the spirit of not allowing the enemy to attack a second time. This is the spirit of forestalling in every sense. Once at the enemy, you should not aspire just to strike him, but to cling after the attack. You must study this deeply. "An example would be attacking the enemy after he misses an attack and is having to reposition his footwork to try again."

To Know "Collapse"

Everything can collapse. Houses, bodies, and enemies collapse when their rhythm becomes deranged. In large-scale strategy, when the enemy starts to collapse you must pursue him without letting the chance go. If you fail to take advantage of your enemies' collapse, they may recover.

In single combat, the enemy sometimes loses timing and collapses. If you let this opportunity pass, he may recover and not be so negligent thereafter. Fix your eye on the enemy's collapse, and chase him, attacking so that you do not let him recover. You must do this. The chasing attack is with a strong spirit. You must utterly cut the enemy down so that he does not recover his position. You must understand utterly how to cut down the enemy. "If the enemy is exhausted or in great pain from your attacks is a great time to take the initiative and finish the fight."

To Become the Enemy

"To become the enemy" means to think yourself into the enemy's position. In the world people tend to think of a robber trapped in a house as a fortified enemy. However, if we think of "becoming the enemy", we feel that the whole world is against us and that there is no escape. He who is shut inside is a pheasant. He who enters to arrest is a hawk. You must appreciate this.

In large-scale strategy, people are always under the impression that the enemy is strong, and so tend to become cautious. But if you have good soldiers, and if you understand the principles of strategy, and if you know how to beat the enemy, there is nothing to worry about.

In single combat also you must put yourself in the enemy's position. If you think, "Here is a master of the Way, who knows the principles of strategy", then you will surely lose. You must consider this deeply. "How does your attacker see you? Are you a threat or easy prey? Use this to your advantage."

To Release Four Hands

"To release four hands" is used when you and the enemy are contending with the same spirit, and the issue cannot be decided. Abandon this spirit and win through an alternative resource. In large-scale strategy, when there is a "four hands" spirit, do not give up — it is

man's existence. Immediately throw away this spirit and win with a technique the enemy does not expect. In single combat also, when we think we have fallen into the "four hands" situation, we must defeat the enemy by changing our mind and applying a suitable technique according to his condition. You must be able to judge this. "In true combat if you cannot win in three strikes, you must change tactics immediately! Anymore and the enemy will have time to gather your timing and spirit. Use one or two speed techniques followed by a strong finishing move."

To Move the Shade

"To move the shade" is used when you cannot see the enemy's spirit. In large-scale strategy, when you cannot see the enemy's position, indicate that you are about to attack strongly, to discover his resources. It is easy then to defeat him with a different method once you see his resources.

In single combat, if the enemy takes up a rear or side attitude of the long sword so that you cannot see his intention, make a feint attack, and the enemy will show his long sword, thinking he sees your spirit. Benefiting from what you are shown, you can win with certainty. If you are negligent you will miss the timing. Research this well. "Use feints to draw the enemy into showing his strengths. This will show you what you need to use to defeat him. Is he a kicker or boxer? Does try to grapple?"

To Hold Down a Shadow

"Holding down a shadow" is used when you can see the enemy's attacking spirit. In large-scale strategy, when the enemy embarks on an attack, if you make a show of strongly suppressing his technique, he will change his mind. Then, altering your spirit, defeat him by forestalling him with a Void spirit.

Or, in single combat, hold down the enemy's strong intention with a suitable timing, and defeat him by forestalling him with this timing. You must study this well.

To Pass On

Many things are said to be passed on. Sleepiness can be passed on, and yawning can be passed on. Time can be passed on also.

In large-scale strategy, when the enemy is agitated and shows an inclination to rush, do not mind in the least. Make a show of complete calmness, and the enemy will be taken by this and will become relaxed. When you see that this spirit has been passed on, you can bring about the enemy's defeat by attacking strongly with a Void spirit.

In single combat, you can win by relaxing your body and spirit and then, catching on the moment the enemy relaxes attack strongly and quickly, forestalling him. What is known as "getting someone drunk" is similar to this. You can also infect the enemy with a bored, careless, or weak spirit. You must study this well. "We can hypnotize the enemy by moving slowly, speaking slowly, and staying calm. The reverse is also true, agitating the enemy by erratic movements and yelling. Think of yawning and how contagious this is. The same is true here. Once you see the enemy relax burst forward and attack strongly."

To Cause Loss of Balance

Many things can cause a loss of balance. One cause is danger, another is hardship, and another is surprise. You must research this.

In large-scale strategy it is important to cause loss of balance. Attack without warning where the enemy is not expecting it, and while his spirit is undecided follow up your advantage and, having the lead, defeat him.

Or, in single combat, start by making a show of being slow, then suddenly attack strongly. Without allowing him space for breath to recover from the fluctuation of spirit, you must grasp the opportunity to win. Get the feel of this. "Making the opponent uncomfortable through fear, excitement, or taking advantage of his emotions."

To Frighten

Fright often occurs, caused by the unexpected. In large-scale strategy you can frighten the enemy not by what you present to their eyes, but by shouting, making a small force seem large, or by threatening them from the flank without warning. These things all frighten. You can win by making best use of the enemy's frightened rhythm.

In single combat, also, you must use the advantage of taking the enemy unawares by frightening him with your body, long sword, or voice, to defeat him. You should research this well.

To Soak In

When you have come to grips and are striving together with the enemy, and you realize that you cannot advance, you "soak in" and become one with the enemy. You can win by applying a suitable technique while you are mutually entangled. In battles involving large numbers as well as in fights with small numbers, you can often win decisively with the advantage of knowing how to "soak" into the enemy, whereas, were you to draw apart, you would lose the chance to win. Research this well.

To Injure the Corners

It is difficult to move strong things by pushing directly, so you should "injure the corners". In large-scale strategy, it is beneficial to strike at the corners of the enemy's force. If the corners are overthrown, the spirit of the whole body will be overthrown. To defeat the enemy you must follow up the attack when the corners have fallen.

In single combat, it is easy to win once the enemy collapses. This happens when you injure the "corners" of his body, and this weakens him. It is important to know how to do this, so you must research this deeply. "The four corners represent the shoulders and hips or knees. By attacking the legs with either kicks or sweeps we remove the foundation. The same is true for attacking the shoulders. In grappling by shoving one shoulder back we break the enemy's balance and therefore his strength. This can also apply to joint breaking and shoulders locks."

To Throw into Confusion

This means making the enemy lose resolve. In large-scale strategy we can use your troops to confuse the enemy on the field. Observing the enemy's spirit, we can make him think, "Here? There? Like that? Like this? Slow? Fast?" Victory is certain when the enemy is caught up in a rhythm that confuses his spirit. In single combat, we can confuse the enemy by attacking with varied techniques when the chance arises. Feint a thrust or cut, or make the enemy think you are going close to him, and when he is confused you can easily win. This is the essence of fighting, and you must research it deeply. "Monkey Kung Fu uses this strategy well. Look side to side erratically while yelling and screaming confuses the opponent as the monkey attacks. Again the use of foul language or even crying can confuse or put him off guard."

The Three Shouts

The three shouts are divided thus: before, during and after. Shout according to the situation. The voice is a thing of life. We shout against fires and so on, against the wind and the waves. The voice shows energy.

In large-scale strategy, at the start of battle we shout as loudly as possible. During the fight, the voice is low-pitched, shouting out as we attack. After the contest, we shout in the wake of our victory. These are the three shouts.

In single combat, we make as if to cut and shout "Ei!" at the same time to disturb the enemy, then in the wake of our shout we cut with the long sword. We shout after we have cut down the enemy — this is to announce victory. This is called "sen go no koe" (before and after voice). We do not shout simultaneously with flourishing the long sword. We shout during the fight to get into rhythm. Research this deeply. "The kia is well known is every martial art. It gives us courage and power while striking. It intimidates the enemy. Sometimes even the use of foul language can intimidate the weak hearted. There are times a kia would not be applicable. Times when the enemy may have friends nearby or we don't want to attack attention. Here a hissing sound of forced breath is more desired. Certain sounds also affect the body giving it power. Such as "Ha!" which affects the heart."

To Mingle

In battles, when the armies are in confrontation, attack the enemy's strong points and, when you see that they are beaten back, quickly separate and attack yet another strong point on the periphery of his force. The spirit of this is like a winding mountain path. This is an important fighting method for one man against many. Strike down the enemies in one quarter, or drive them back, and then grasp the timing and attack further strong points to right and left, as if on a winding mountain path, weighing up the enemies' disposition. When you know the enemies' level, attack strongly with no trace of retreating spirit.

In single combat, too, use this spirit with the enemy's strong points. What is meant by 'mingling' is the spirit of advancing and becoming engaged with the enemy, and not withdrawing even one step. You must understand this. "Bagua is well known for this. The weaving of the eight directions of attacks. The Bagua stylist weaves in and around his opponents using them as shields as he attacks his friends."

To Crush

This means to crush the enemy regarding him as being weak. In large-scale strategy, when we see that the enemy has few men, or if he has many men but his spirit is weak and disordered, we knock the hat over his eyes, crushing him utterly. If we crush lightly, he may recover. You must learn the spirit of crushing as if with a hand-grip.

In single combat, if the enemy is less skillful than you, if his rhythm is disorganized, or if he has fallen into evasive or retreating attitudes, we must crush him straightaway, with no concern for his presence and without allowing him space for breath. It is essential to crush him all at once. The primary thing is not to let him recover his position even a little. You must research this deeply. "Mock the opponent after defeating or when he is in pain or on the verge of giving up. Defeat his spirit to win."

The Mountain-Sea Change

The "mountain-sea" spirit means that it is bad to repeat the same thing several times when fighting the enemy. There may be no help but to do something twice, but do not try it a third time. If you once make an attack and fail, there is little chance of success if you use the same approach again. If you attempt a technique which you have previously tried unsuccessfully and fail yet again, then you must change your attacking method.

If the enemy thinks of the mountains, attack like the sea; and if he thinks of the sea, attack like the mountains. You must research this deeply. "If you cannot win with three strikes you need to change strategy right away. Using the same strategy when it is not working will give the opponent time to pick up on your timing."

To Penetrate the Depths

When we are fighting with the enemy, even when it can be seen that we can win on the surface with the benefit of the Way, if his spirit is not extinguished, he may be beaten superficially yet undefeated in spirit deep inside. With this principle of "penetrating the depths" we can destroy the enemy's spirit in its depths, demoralizing him by quickly changing our spirit. This often occurs. Penetrating the depths means penetrating with the long sword, penetrating with the body, and penetrating with the spirit. This cannot be understood in a generalization. Once we have crushed the enemy in the depths, there is no need to remain spirited. But otherwise we must remain spirited. If the enemy remains spirited it is difficult to crush him. You must train in penetrating the depths for large-scale strategy and also single combat. "Again the use of mocking or foul language or gestures, making him lose the will to win. In military strategy this is called "harass and interdiction." Keeping the opponent from resting, getting his balance, or keeping his confidence up will allow you to win easily."

To Renew

"To renew" applies when we are fighting with the enemy, and an entangled spirit arises where there is no possible resolution. We must abandon our efforts, think of the situation in a fresh spirit then win in the new rhythm. To renew, when we are deadlocked with the enemy, means that without changing our circumstance we change our spirit and win through a different technique. It is necessary to consider how "to renew" also applies in large-scale strategy. Research this diligently. "Learn to switch from one element to the next as needed. Earth when we are stronger, water when we need to flank and counter, fire when we are in control and need to be aggressive. The elements change as the situation does. Staying in a fire element when it is not needed may give us more trouble than wanted. Do we really need to fight this person? Is our life at stake? Is there more than one? Has this person just had too many drinks? Each element teaches us how to react in various situations."

Rat's Head, Ox's Neck

"Rat's head and ox's neck" means that, when we are fighting with the enemy and both he and we have become occupied with small points in an entangled spirit, we must always think of the Way of strategy as being both a rat's head and an ox's neck. Whenever we have become preoccupied with small details, we must suddenly change into a large spirit, interchanging large with small. This is one of the essences of strategy. It is necessary that the warrior think in this spirit in everyday life. You must not depart from this spirit in large-scale strategy nor in single combat.

The Commander Knows the Troops

"The commander knows the troops" applies everywhere in fights in my Way of strategy. Using the wisdom of strategy, think of the enemy as your own troops. When you think in this way you can move him at will and be able to chase him around. You become the general and the enemy becomes your troops. You must master this. "Learn about yourself. What makes you angry? What are you afraid of? What excites you etc? By learning these things about yourself you can understand others. This in return will allow you to control them."

To Let Go the Hilt

There are various kinds of spirit involved in letting go the hilt. There is the spirit of winning without a sword. There is also the spirit of holding the long sword but not winning. The various methods cannot be expressed in writing. You must train well. "Fights can sometimes be won with just a look. Developing the spirit will allow this. Some arts teach this as a meditation. These are known as "Shen Gong."

The Body of a Rock

When you have mastered the Way of strategy you can suddenly make your body like a rock, and ten thousand things cannot touch you. This is the body of a rock. You will not be moved. Oral tradition. "A quick method of Iron body can be done as the opponent is striking. As he strikes tuck the hips under while sinking the mind into the Earth. This takes the energy from the strike and moves it to the ground."

What is recorded above is what has been constantly on my mind about Ichi school sword fencing, written down as it came to me. This is the first time I have written about my technique, and the order of things is a bit confused. It is difficult to express it clearly.

This book is a spiritual guide for the man who wishes to learn the Way. My heart has been inclined to the Way of strategy from my youth onwards. I have devoted myself to training my hand, tempering my body, and attaining the many spiritual attitudes of sword fencing. If we watch men of other schools discussing theory, and concentrating on techniques with the hands, even though they seem skillful to watch, they have not the slightest true spirit.

Of course, men who study in this way think they are training the body and spirit, but it is an obstacle to the true Way, and its bad influence remains forever. Thus the true Way of strategy is becoming decadent and dying the true Way of sword fencing is the craft of defeating the enemy in a fight, and nothing other than this. If you attain and adhere to the wisdom of my strategy, you need never doubt that you will win.

The second year of Shoho, the fifth month, the twelfth day (1645)

Teruo Magonojo SHINMEN MUSASHI

The Wind Book

In strategy you must know the Ways of other schools, so I have written about various other traditions of strategy in this the Wind Book. Without knowledge of the Ways of other schools, it is difficult to understand the essence of my Ichi school. Looking at other schools we find some that specialize in techniques of strength using extra-long swords. Some schools study the Way of the short sword, known as kodachi. Some schools teach dexterity in large numbers of sword techniques, teaching attitudes of the sword as the "surface" and the Way as the "interior".

That none of these are the true Way I show clearly in the interior of this book — all the vices and virtues and rights and wrongs. My Ichi School is different. Other schools make accomplishments their means of livelihood, growing flowers and decoratively coloring articles in order to sell them. "Today many schools teach flashy nontraditional forms or techniques in order to win tournaments. This is only to impress the judges. Not true martial arts and only to make money by gaining more students." This is definitely not the Way of strategy.

Some of the world's strategists are concerned only with sword fencing, and limit their training to flourishing the long sword and carriage of the body. But is dexterity alone sufficient to win? This is not the essence of the Way.

I have recorded the unsatisfactory points of other schools one by one in this book. You must study these matters deeply to appreciate the benefit of my Ni To Ichi school.

Other Schools Using Extra-Long Swords

Some other schools have a liking for extra-long swords. From the point of view of my strategy these must be seen as weak schools. This is because they do not appreciate the principle of cutting the enemy by any means. Their preference is for the extra-long sword and, relying on the virtue of its length, they think to defeat the enemy from a distance. "The use of heavy or extra-long weapons is used in many arts. This strengthens the muscles and tendons and teaches the student to extend the chi beyond the hands."

In this world it is said, "One inch gives the hand advantage", but these are the idle words of one who does not know strategy. It shows the inferior strategy of a weak sprit that men should be dependent on the length of their sword, fighting from a distance without the benefit of strategy.

I expect there is a case for the school in question liking extra-long swords as part of its doctrine, but if we compare this with real life it is unreasonable. Surely we need not necessarily be defeated if we are using a short sword, and have no long sword? It is difficult for these people to cut the enemy when at close quarters because of the length of the long sword. The blade path is large so the long sword is an encumbrance, and they are at a disadvantage compared to the man armed with a short companion sword. "Practice with long range and short."

From olden times it has been said: "Great and small go together." So do not unconditionally dislike extra-long swords. What I dislike is the inclination towards the long sword. If we consider large-scale strategy, we can think of large forces in terms of long swords, and small forces as short swords. Cannot few men give battle against many? There are many instances of few men overcoming many.

Your strategy is of no account if when called on to fight in a confined space your heart is inclined to the long sword, or if you are in a house armed only with your companion sword. Besides, some men have not the strength of others. In my doctrine, I dislike preconceived, narrow spirit. You must study this well.

The Strong Long Sword Spirit in Other Schools

You should not speak of strong and weak long swords. If you just wield the long sword in a strong spirit your cutting will become coarse, and if you use the sword coarsely you will have difficulty in winning. If you are concerned with the strength of your sword, you will try to cut unreasonably strongly, and will not be able to cut at all. It is also bad to try to cut strongly when testing the sword. Whenever you cross swords with an enemy you must not think of cutting him either strongly or weakly; just think of cutting and killing him. Be intent solely on killing the enemy. Do not try to cut strongly and, of course, do not think of cutting weakly. You should only be concerned with killing the enemy.

If you rely on strength, when you hit the enemy's sword you will inevitably hit too hard. If you do this, your own sword will be carried along as a result. Thus the saying, "The strongest hand wins", has no meaning. In large-scale strategy, if you have a strong army and are relying on strength to win, but the enemy also has a strong army, the battle will be fierce. This is the same for both sides. Without the correct principle the fight cannot be won.

The spirit of my school is to win through the wisdom of strategy, paying no attention to trifles. Study this well.

Use of the Shorter Long Sword in Other Schools

In ancient times, tachi and katana meant long and short swords. Men of superior strength in the world can wield even a long sword lightly, so there is no case for their liking the short sword. They also make use of the length of spears and halberds. Some men use a shorter long sword with the intention of jumping in and stabbing the enemy at the unguarded moment when he flourishes his sword. This inclination is bad.

To aim for the enemy's unguarded moment is completely defensive and undesirable at close quarters with the enemy. Furthermore, you cannot use the method of jumping inside his defense with a short sword if there are many enemies. Some men think that if they go against many enemies with a shorter long sword they can unrestrictedly frisk around cutting in sweeps, but they have to parry cuts continuously, and eventually become entangled with the enemy. This is inconsistent with the true Way of strategy.

The sure Way to win thus is to chase the enemy around in a confusing manner, causing him to jump aside, with your body held strongly and straight. The same principle applies to large-scale strategy. The essence of strategy is to fall upon the enemy in large numbers and to bring about his speedy downfall. By their study of strategy, people of the world get used to countering, evading and retreating as the normal thing. They become set in this habit, so can easily be paraded around by the enemy. The Way of strategy is straight and true. You must chase the enemy around and make him obey your spirit. "Make him fight your fight. If you don't like defending against kicks, attack his legs until he no longer kicks. Punch the arms of the boxers. "Defang the snake."

Other Schools with many Methods of using the Long Sword. I think it is held in other schools that there are many methods of using the long sword in order to gain the admiration of beginners. This is selling the Way. It is a vile spirit in strategy. The reason for this is that to deliberate over many ways of cutting down a man is an error. To start with, killing is not the Way of mankind. Killing is the same for people who know about fighting and for those who do not. It is the same for women or children, and there are not many different methods. We can speak of different tactics such as stabbing and mowing down, but none other than these.

Anyway, cutting down the enemy is the Way of strategy, and there is no need for many refinements of it. Even so, according to the place, your long sword may be obstructed above or to the sides, so you will need to hold your sword in such manner that it can be used. There are five methods in five directions.

Methods apart from these five hand twisting, body bending, jumping out, and so on, to cut the enemy — are not the true Way of strategy. In order to cut the enemy you must not make twisting or bending cuts. This is completely useless. "In Kung Fu and other arts, the use of bending, jumping, or twisting is of great benefit. It allows the practitioner to strike from unusual angles and even when off balance." In my strategy, I bear my spirit and body straight, and cause the enemy to twist and bend. The necessary spirit is to win by attacking the enemy when his spirit is warped. You must study this well.

Use of Attitudes of the Long Sword in Other Schools

Placing a great deal of importance on the attitudes of the long sword is a mistaken way of thinking. What is known in the world as "attitude" applies when there is no enemy. The reason is that this has been a precedent since ancient times, that there should be no such thing as "This is the modern way to do it" dueling. You must force the enemy into inconvenient situations. Attitudes are for situations in which you are not to be moved. That is, for garrisoning castles, battle array, and so on, showing the spirit of not being moved even by a strong assault. In the Way of dueling, however, you must always be intent upon taking the lead and attacking. Attitude is the spirit of awaiting an attack. You must appreciate this. "Attitudes can also be called Shadows or stances. We must not think of stances as stationary but moving. We do not adopt a stance and fight from it but rather we move to it while defending or attacking. The stance is dictated by our opponent actions."

In duels of strategy you must move the opponent's attitude. Attack where his spirit is lax, throw him into confusion, irritate and terrify him. Take advantage of the enemy's rhythm when he is unsettled and you can win.

I dislike the defensive spirit known as "attitude". Therefore, in my Way, there is something called "Attitude-No Attitude". In large-scale strategy we deploy our troops for battle bearing in mind our strength, observing the enemy's numbers, and noting the details of the battlefield. This is at the start of the battle.

The spirit of attacking is completely different from the spirit of being attacked. Bearing an attack well, with a strong attitude, and parrying the enemy's attack well, is like making a wall of spears and halberds. When you attack the enemy, your spirit must go to the extent of pulling the stakes out of a wall and using them as spears and halberds. You must examine this well.

Fixing the Eyes in Other Schools

Some schools maintain that the eyes should be fixed on the enemy's long sword. Some schools fix the eye on the hands. Some fix the eyes on the face, and some fix the eyes on the feet, and so on. If you fix the eyes on these places your spirit can become confused, and your strategy thwarted. I will explain this in detail. Footballer do not fix their eyes on the ball, but by good play on the field they can perform well. When you become accustomed to something, you are not limited to the use of your eyes. People such as master musicians have the music score in front of their nose, or flourish the sword in several ways when they have mastered the Way, but this does not mean that they fix their eyes on these things specifically, or that they make pointless movements of the sword. It means that they can see naturally. "Sometimes during stress we develop tunnel vision which can allow us to be attacked from outside or sight. Our gaze needs to allow us to see not only forward but to the left and right as well. Qigong meditations train this type of gaze. While fighting only one opponent, the gaze should allow you to see from the shoulders to the feet. Watch the shoulders and knees for this is where all movements originate."

In the Way of strategy, when you have fought many times you will easily be able to appraise the speed and position of the enemy's sword, and having mastery of the Way you will see the weight of his spirit. In strategy, fixing the eyes means gazing at the man's heart.

In large-scale strategy the area to watch is the enemy's strength. "Perception" and "sight" are the two methods of seeing. Perception consists of concentrating strongly on the enemy's spirit, observing the condition of the battle field, fixing the gaze strongly, seeing the progress of the fight and the changes of advantage. This is the sure way to win.

In single combat you must not fix the eyes on details. As I said before, if you fix your eyes on details and neglect important things, your spirit will become bewildered, and victory will escape you. Research this principle well and train diligently.

Use of the Feet in Other Schools

There are various methods of using the feet: floating foot, jumping foot, springing foot, treading foot, crow's foot, and such nimble walking methods. From the point of view of my strategy, these are all unsatisfactory. I dislike floating foot because the feet always tend to float during the fight. The Way must be trod firmly.

Neither do I like jumping foot, because it encourages the habit of jumping, and a jumpy spirit. However much you jump, there is no real justification for it, so jumping is bad. Springing foot causes a springing spirit which is indecisive. Treading foot is a "waiting" method, and I especially dislike it.

Apart from these, there are various fast walking methods, such as crow's foot, and so on Sometimes, however, you may encounter the enemy on marshland, swampy ground, river valleys, stony ground, or narrow roads, in which situations you cannot jump or move the feet quickly.

In my strategy, the footwork does not change. I always walk as I usually do in the street. You must never lose control of your feet. According to the enemy's rhythm, move fast or slowly, adjusting your body not too much and not too little.

Carrying the feet is important also in large-scale strategy. This is because, if you attack quickly and thoughtlessly without knowing the enemy's spirit, your rhythm will become deranged and you will not be able to win. Or, if you advance too slowly, you will not be able to take advantage of the enemy's disorder, the opportunity to win will escape, and you will not be able to finish the fight quickly. You must win by seizing upon the enemy's disorder and derangement, and by not according him even a little hope of recovery. Practice this well. "Practice of various footwork patterns can eventually become our natural everyday way of moving."

Speed in Other Schools

Speed is not part of the true Way of strategy. Speed implies that things seem fast or slow, according to whether or not they are in rhythm. Whatever the Way, the master of strategy does not appear fast.

Some people can walk as fast as a hundred or a hundred and twenty miles in a day, but this does not mean that they run continuously from morning till night. Unpracticed runners may seem to have been running all day, but their performance is poor. "Timing and reception is always more important than speed."

In the Way of dance, accomplished performers can sing while dancing, but when beginners try this they slow down and their spirit becomes busy. The "old pine tree"^^ melody beaten on a leather drum is tranquil, but when beginners try this they slow down and their spirit becomes busy. Very skillful people can manage a fast rhythm, but it is bad to beat hurriedly. If you try to beat too quickly you will get out of time. Of course, slowness is bad. Really skillful people never get out of time, and are always deliberate, and never appear busy. From this example, the principle can be seen.

What is known as speed is especially bad in the Way of strategy. The reason for this is that depending on the place, marsh or swamp and so on, it may not be possible to move the body and legs together quickly. Still less will you be able to cut quickly if you have a long sword in this situation. If you try to cut quickly, as if using a fan or short sword, you will not actually cut even a little. You must appreciate this.

In large-scale strategy also, a fast busy spirit is undesirable. The spirit must be that of holding down a pillow, and then you will not be even a little late. When you opponent is hurrying recklessly, you must act contrarily, and keep calm. You must not be influenced by the opponent. Train diligently to attain this spirit.

Interior" and "Surface" in Other Schools

There is no "interior" or "surface" in strategy. The artistic accomplishments usually claim inner meaning and secret tradition, and "interior" and "gate","' but in combat there is no such thing as fighting on the surface, or cutting with the interior. When I teach my Way, I first teach by training in techniques which are easy for the pupil to understand, a doctrine which is easy to understand. I gradually endeavor to explain the deep principle, points which it is hardly possible to comprehend, according to the pupil's progress. In any event, because the way to understanding is through experience, I do not speak of "interior" and "gate".

In this world, if you go into the mountains, and decide to go deeper and yet deeper, instead you will emerge at the gate. Whatever is the Way, it has an interior, and it is sometimes a good thing to point out the gate. In strategy, we cannot say what is concealed and what is revealed. "In traditional martial we teach the same way. Students are taught things that are easily learned and understood. As their wisdom grows more advanced techniques are taught. In Chinese the word "Men" means gate or door. This door is closed to all but the most worthy students. This is where the true arts are taught."

Accordingly I dislike passing on my Way through written pledges and regulations. Perceiving the ability of my pupils, I teach the direct Way, remove the bad influence of other schools, and gradually introduce them to the true Way of the warrior.

The method of teaching my strategy is with a trustworthy thy spirit. You must train diligently. I have tried to record an outline of the strategy of other schools in the above nine sections. I could now continue by giving a specific account of these schools one by one, from the "gate" to the "interior", but I have intentionally not named the schools or their main points. The reason for this is that different branches of schools give different interpretations of the doctrines. In as much as men's opinions differ, so there must be differing ideas on the same matter. Thus no one man's conception is valid for any school. I have shown the general tendencies of other schools on nine points. If we look at them from an honest viewpoint, we see that people always tend to like long swords or short swords, and become concerned with strength in both large and small matters. You can see why I do not deal with the "gates" of other schools.

In my Ichi school of the long sword there is neither gate nor interior. There is no inner meaning in sword attitudes. You must simply keep your spirit true to realize the virtue of strategy.

Twelfth day of the fifth month, the second year of Shoho (1645)

Teruo Magonojo SHINMEN MUSASHI

The Book of the Void

The Ni To Ichi Way of strategy is recorded in this the Book of the Void. What is called the spirit of the void is where there is nothing. It is not included in man's knowledge. Of course the void is nothingness. By knowing things that exist, you can know that which does not exist. That is the void. People in this world look at things mistakenly, and think that what they do not understand must be the void. This is not the true void. It is bewilderment. "In Kung Fu we might think of the void as where the other four elements are created and return."

In the Way of strategy, also, those who study as warriors think that whatever they cannot understand in their craft is the void. This is not the true void. To attain the Way of strategy as a warrior you must study fully other martial arts and not deviate even a little from the Way of the warrior. With your spirit settled, accumulate practice day by day, and hour by hour. Polish the twofold spirit heart and mind, and sharpen the twofold gaze perception and sight. When your spirit is not in the least clouded, when the clouds of bewilderment clear away, there is the true void.

Until you realize the true Way, whether in Buddhism or in common sense, you may think that things are correct and in order. However, if we look at things objectively, from the viewpoint of laws of the world, we see various doctrines departing from the true Way. Know well this spirit, and with forthrightness as the foundation and the true spirit as the Way. Enact strategy broadly, correctly and openly. Then you will come to think of things in a wide sense and, taking the void as the Way, you will see the Way as void. In the void is virtue, and no evil. Wisdom has existence, principle has existence, the Way has existence, and spirit is nothingness. "Our training should start as something special but eventually return to our original state and be natural to us."

Twelfth day of the fifth month, second year of Shoho (1645)

Teruo Magonojo SHINMEN MUSASHI

Made in the USA
Middletown, DE
18 February 2018